GUYANA

...in Pictures

Independent Picture Service

GUYANA
...in Pictures

Prepared by
Geography Department

34557

Lerner Publications Company
Minneapolis

Courtesy of Patricia Koopmans

Most Guyanese houses are raised on stilts to prevent damage to buildings from frequent flooding.

This book is an all-new edition in the Visual Geography Series. Previous editions were published by Sterling Publishing Company, New York City. The text, set in 10/12 Century Textbook, is fully revised and updated, and new photographs, maps, charts, and captions have been added.

LIBRARY OF CONGRESS CATALOGING-IN-PUBLICATION DATA

Guyana in pictures.

(Visual geography series)
Rev. ed. of: Guyana in pictures / Charles F. Gritzner.
Includes index.
Summary: Text and illustrations introduce the geography, history, government, people, and economy of the South American republic once known as British Guiana.
1. Guyana. [1. Guyana] I. Gritzner, Charles F. Guyana in pictures. II. Lerner Publications Company. Geography Dept. III. Visual geography series (Minneapolis, Minn.)
F2368.G9   1988   988.1   87-2797
ISBN 0-8225-1815-5 (lib. bdg.)

International Standard Book Number: 0-8225-1815-5
Library of Congress Catalog Card Number: 87-2797

VISUAL GEOGRAPHY SERIES®

Publisher
Harry Jonas Lerner
Associate Publisher
Nancy M. Campbell
Executive Series Editor
Mary M. Rodgers
Assistant Series Editor
Gretchen Bratvold
Editorial Assistant
Nora W. Kniskern
Illustrations Editors
Nathan A. Haverstock
Karen A. Sirvaitis
Consultants/Contributors
Dr. Ruth F. Hale
Nathan A. Haverstock
Sandra K. Davis
Designer
Jim Simondet
Cartographer
Carol F. Barrett
Indexer
Kristine I. Spangard
Production Manager
Gary J. Hansen

Courtesy of Patricia Koopmans

Guyanese schoolgirls compete in a sack race.

Acknowledgments

Title page photo courtesy of Consulate General of the Republic of Guyana.

Elevation contours adapted from *The Times Atlas of the World,* seventh comprehensive edition (New York: Times Books, 1985).

4 5 6 7 8 9 10 — JR — 03 02 01 00 99 98 97

During Guyana's short dry season, a worker labors to harvest the rice crop.

Contents

VENEZUELA

ATLANTIC OCEAN

Port
Kaituma

Barima R.

Waini R.

Charity

Anna Regina

Pomeroon R.

LEGUAN ISLAND

GEORGETOWN

Cuyuni R.

Timehri
Airport

New Amsterdam

Bartica

Mazaruni R.

Abary R.

Everton

MAZARUNI

Linden

Corriverton

Essequibo R.

Demerara R.

DIAMOND

Canje R.

FIELDS

Ituni

Potaro R.

Berbice R.

KAIETEUR FALLS

Courantyne R.

BRAZIL

Rupununi R.

Tacutu R.

GUYANA

Agricultural Districts

N

| 0 | | 50 | | 100 | Miles |
| 0 | 50 | | 100 | Kilometers | |

SURINAME

Boundary Disputed

80°   60°   40°

EQUATOR

0°   0°

PACIFIC
OCEAN

20°

GUYANA

SOUTH AMERICA

ATLANTIC
40°

OCEAN

0   1000   Miles
0   1000   Kilometers

METRIC CONVERSION CHART
To Find Approximate Equivalents

WHEN YOU KNOW:	MULTIPLY BY:	TO FIND:
AREA		
acres	0.41	hectares
square miles	2.59	square kilometers
CAPACITY		
gallons	3.79	liters
LENGTH		
feet	30.48	centimeters
yards	0.91	meters
miles	1.61	kilometers
MASS (weight)		
pounds	0.45	kilograms
tons	0.91	metric tons
VOLUME		
cubic yards	0.77	cubic meters
TEMPERATURE		
degrees Fahrenheit	0.56 (after subtracting 32)	degrees Celsius

A high school volleyball team—traveling along the coast between the Essequibo River and Georgetown to play in local tournaments—reflects the ethnic diversity of Guyana's population.

Introduction

Upon achieving independence from Great Britain in 1966, Guyana found itself sharply divided between two groups of Guyanese citizens—those of East Indian roots and those of African ancestry. At times this ethnic mixture has caused great national tension and political strife.

In 1970 Guyana embodied its hopes for unity and progress in a cooperative, socialist form of government. By officially becoming the Cooperative Republic of Guyana, the nation declared its intention to pull together the resources of its

people and its land. This formal recognition of the spirit of combined effort was unique and resulted in the nationalization of most of Guyana's industries.

By the late 1980s, however, Guyana had replaced Haiti as the poorest nation in Latin America. To save the deteriorating economy, Guyana's leaders revised the country's socialist goals. Some formerly government-owned industries are now slowly being turned over to private interests.

Reform of the country's political system has also taken place. In 1992, after the

7

Guyanese government drew up new voter lists, the nation held a presidential election. Although violence marred the voting, most observers believed the election had been fair. A new political party took power, and the Guyanese hope that democracy has finally been established in their country.

In building their nation, the Guyanese draw upon a varied history. Early Spanish explorers believed that the region was the likely location of El Dorado, a legendary land of golden riches. The Dutch, who arrived in the seventeenth century to establish a colony, discovered the great fertility of the soil along Guyana's Atlantic coast.

British planters followed the Dutch settlers, and both European groups fostered the development of a slave-based plantation economy. Guyana's present-day citizens of African descent claim their ancestry from this enslaved labor force.

With the abolition of slavery in all British colonies in 1834, the planters shifted to a new method of obtaining low-cost labor, called the indenture (contract) system. Under this format, the East Indian population in Guyana had its beginning.

Despite Guyana's location on the northern coast of South America, its economy resembles the commercial structures of Caribbean countries more than the economies of South American nations. Consequently, Guyana is a member of both the Caribbean Community and the Caribbean Development Bank.

Like most of Latin America, however, Guyana has a complex racial and cultural history. The nation's greatest challenges lie in forging a single identity out of its diverse ethnic groups and religions and in overcoming a colonial past that was often bitter and oppressive.

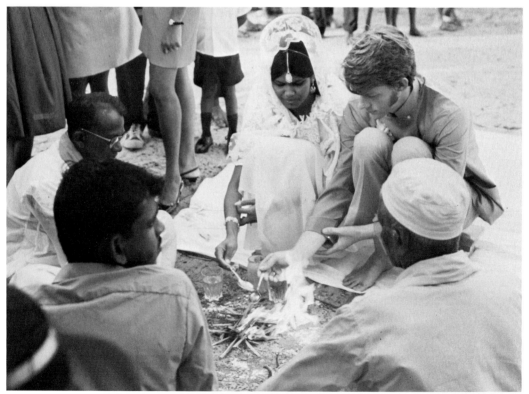

Courtesy of Patricia Koopmans

As part of a Hindu wedding ritual, the couple jointly place their offerings in a ceremonial fire.

Courtesy of Consulate General of the Republic of Guyana

Mount Roraima—which, at 9,094 feet, is the highest peak in Guyana—stands where the nation's borders meet those of Brazil and Venezuela.

1) The Land

The Cooperative Republic of Guyana—formerly the colony of British Guiana—occupies 83,000 square miles of territory on the northeastern coast of South America. Slightly smaller than the state of Minnesota, Guyana is bounded on the west by Venezuela, on the southwest by Brazil, and on the east by Suriname. Its northern boundary consists of 270 miles of coastline on the Atlantic Ocean.

Guyana is an Indian word that means "land of [many] waters." The Europeans first used the name to refer to the triangle formed by the Orinoco, Amazon, and Negro rivers. The British used "Guiana" —an English spelling of the same Indian name—to refer to their New World colony.

With the coming of the Europeans, the triangular region was politically subdivided. The portion of Venezuela located south of the Orinoco River was known as Spanish Guiana, while the part sited north of the Amazon was called Portuguese

Guiana. Also in this region were British Guiana, Dutch Guiana (now independent Suriname), and French Guiana, which is still a French colony.

Topography

Guyana's landscape begins with a flat coastal strip, followed by a belt of rolling hills, and ends in the interior highlands. These separate topographical features appear as three broad steps, with each one becoming higher and less accessible as the distance from the coast increases.

On a map, Guyana's rivers look like giant fallen trees. The main channels, which flow into the Atlantic Ocean, represent the trunks, and the thousands of tributaries that drain the highlands form the branches. As these streams flow through the varied countryside, spectacular waterfalls appear along the upper stream courses, and rapids endanger navigation on the lower reaches of the rivers.

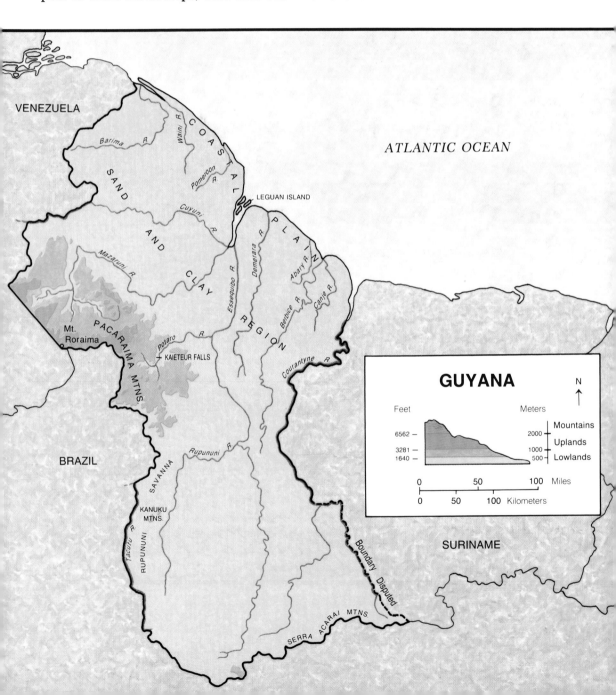

Courtesy of Patricia Koopmans

The waves of the Atlantic Ocean break against a seawall that protects the coastal plain from excessive soil erosion.

Coastal Plain

Guyana's population is concentrated in a 10- to 40-mile-wide coastal plain facing the Atlantic Ocean. This region occupies less than 5 percent of Guyana's total national territory, yet it supports almost 90 percent of the population. Nearly all the country's agricultural production is centered in this area, which is well served by Guyana's land transportation network.

The coastal plain is a varied region of mud flats and beach ridges, which run parallel to the coast and are separated by low areas of marsh and swamp. This land is literally a gift of the water, because it has been built up over thousands of years by sand, silt, and clay deposited by the rivers and the ocean. The many rivers that originate in the highlands have transported these materials to the sea.

Courtesy of Patricia Koopmans

Flooding hampers movement all along Guyana's coastline. The settlement of Anna Regina (Queen Anne) lies largely underwater after a heavy storm.

Seawalls are an essential tool in Guyana's complex scheme to keep the Atlantic Ocean at bay.

Ironically, the forces of river and sea that have combined to create the highly fertile coastal plain also pose the greatest threat to human settlement and land use. Upon reaching the coast, the sediments carried by the rivers are further moved by waves and coastal currents and are redeposited along the shoreline. The amount of erosion caused by the sea is greater than the amount of deposits brought in from the sea, causing much of the coastal land to erode to below sea level.

In some areas, farms and homes are as much as five feet below sea level. Nearly all of these areas would flood if protective, artificial works that hold back the water did not exist. A system of dams, 140 miles of ocean-facing seawall, and a network of drainage canals had to be completed before the land was suitable for habitation.

Tides, Rivers, and Navigation

The coast of Guyana experiences spring tides measuring up to eight feet in height. During high tide, much of the unprotected coastal plain is flooded by sea water. A rising tide in this area is also responsible for an interesting phenomenon known as the "tidal bore"—a surge of water that flows upstream, sometimes for as much as 60 miles. When the tidal bore occurs, the upstream force is so great that it is impossible to paddle a canoe downstream against the incoming current. When the tide reverses, the streams carry not only their normal freshwater volume, but additional salt water as well. With the greater volume of water, the current flows more quickly than usual.

Local river navigation is carefully scheduled to take advantage of the tidal changes. Navigation by large vessels—either along the coast or on the lower stream courses—is severely limited during low tides. Sandbars and mud flats can also pose a hazard for as much as 15 miles inland from the coastline.

At high tide, boatmen skillfully take advantage of local currents and increased water volume to navigate Guyana's streams.

Tidal movements pile sand into mounds that eventually may break the surface of the water. The mounds — called sandbars — block navigation along the coast.

Northern Guyana – with its heavy rainfall and nearness to the sea – needs extensive irrigation and drainage works, such as those in the Abary River system, to control the incoming water and to put it to agricultural use.

14

Large ships can navigate the major rivers only as far inland as the first rapids. Along most of the streams, the rapids generally appear at the point downstream where the rivers enter the coastal lowland. The Essequibo River is navigable for 40 miles upstream from its mouth on the Atlantic Ocean, while the Courantyne and Demerara rivers are traversable for 60 miles. The Berbice River can be traveled for 100 miles of its 370-mile length. Above the rapids of these rivers, however, navigation is limited to shallow boats and dugout canoes.

Sand and Clay Region

Inland from the coastal plain is a 150-mile-wide belt of low, gently rolling terrain characterized by a soil mixture of white sand and clay. Here and there granite hills rise on the horizon. The coarse-grained sand is the weathered and eroded remnant of these granite formations. The clay, on the other hand, was formed by the deposit of fine silts during an earlier geologic period when the area bordered the coast.

This region supports much of the dense, tropical rain-forest of Guyana. Most of the country's mineral wealth is also located here. In a number of locations, wide areas of the earth's surface are mined to reach rich deposits of bauxite (from which aluminum is made). Good quantities of gold, diamonds, and manganese are also found in the region, as well as smaller quantities of other ores.

Interior Highlands

The highest of the three topographical levels comprises a series of flat-topped mountains and plateaus, which range in elevation from about 1,000 to over 9,000 feet. The Pacaraima Mountains in the western interior are the largest range, both in area and in elevation. The range's highest peak—and the tallest point in the country—is Mount Roraima, which rises to

Courtesy of Patricia Koopmans

Small rivers and streams water many parts of Guyana.

Courtesy of Patricia Koopmans

The Tacutu River marks the boundary between Brazil and Guyana.

Courtesy of Patricia Koopmans

9,094 feet. In the far south, near the Brazilian border, are the Kanuku Mountains and the Serra Acaraí. These mountains are exposed remnants of ancient, crystalline rock—some of the oldest sedimentary material in the Western Hemisphere.

While the waterfalls and rapids of the interior highlands limit river navigation, they provide the country with both hydroelectric potential and spectacular scenery. Beautiful Kaieteur Falls on the Potaro River—a western tributary of the Essequibo—have a sheer drop of 741 feet, which is nearly five times greater than the descent of Niagara Falls.

Rainfall and Climate

Guyana's temperatures reflect the climate of both the tropical rain-forest and the tropical savanna, or grassland. Among Guyana's climatic characteristics are heavy rainfall, high humidity, hot temperatures —with greater differences between day and night than between seasons—and steady winds that blow from the northeast during most of the year.

Rainfall varies from an average of over 80 inches a year in parts of the interior highlands to about 60 inches in the Rupununi region. The capital city of Georgetown on the coastal plain, however, receives an annual average of 90 inches of rain. These rainfall fluctuations are of critical importance to farmers, whose crops may fail due to drought in some years and to excessive moisture at other times. During periods of severe drought, forest fires also pose a threat to crops in some parts of the country.

Rainfall normally occurs in relatively short storms during the afternoon. Nearly half of the precipitation pours down during the rainy season from mid-April

Sugarcane is harvested in the autumn months of September and October, when the land is driest.

through mid-August. Another one-quarter of the annual rain falls during a shorter wet season from December through mid-February. The driest period in Guyana is from September through November, during which time the country's major crops—sugarcane and rice—are gathered. Excessive moisture during harvest can cause serious crop losses.

Average temperatures in Georgetown—annually about 80° F—are typical of the coastal region. In the interior, far removed from the moderating influence of the sea, temperatures have reached highs of 103° F in the relatively dry Rupununi region. Lows have been around 60° F in the highlands. The hottest months—September and October—coincide with the period of minimum rainfall.

The long rainy season in Guyana turns a village street into a shallow stream.

17

Flora

Natural vegetation in Guyana reflects differences in rainfall, drainage, soil, and human activity. There are three major botanical regions—the coastal region, the interior forests, and the savannas.

COASTAL VEGETATION

Under natural conditions, the vegetation of the low-lying coastal plain forms an extremely complex mixture of trees and grasses adapted to differences in the elevation, drainage, and salt content of the soil. As a general pattern, coastal mangrove swamps and salt-tolerant marsh grasses merge gradually with inland freshwater marshes and heavily wooded swamps. As elevation increases and drainage improves, dry woodlands and savannas begin to appear. Throughout much of the coastal plain, the clearing of land for settlement and agriculture has changed the patterns of natural vegetation.

INTERIOR FORESTS

Over 70 percent of Guyana's territory consists of dense stands of untouched tropical rain-forest. Giant trees reach upward to 200 feet in height to compete for sunlight. Their broad trunks may measure over 20 feet in diameter, and vines, called lianas, encircle the high branches. Many varieties of epiphytes—vegetation that grows on a host plant but takes its nourishment from the air and rain—are often visible. These epiphytes include numerous bromeliads (plants of the pineapple family) and orchids, as well as thousands of species of smaller plants. All of the lush greenery presents an awesome collection of natural beauty.

SAVANNAS

In the southern interior, between the upper Essequibo River and the Brazilian border, lies the Rupununi Savanna. Made up of sparse grasses, occasional palm trees, and forests, the Rupununi region, which is partially watered by the Rupununi River,

Courtesy of Patricia Koopmans

Famous among water lilies is Guyana's national flower, the *Victoria regis,* whose leaves can reach widths of 10 feet. Found mostly in tranquil ponds, the lily takes its nutrients through air passages that extend down the stems of the leaves.

is the center of Guyana's limited cattle industry. The grazing capacity of the nation's pastureland is severely limited by the poor nutritional content of the native grasses. Conditions have improved somewhat during recent years with the introduction of more nutritious grasses from other countries, particularly from Australia.

Fauna

In terms of both species and actual numbers, nearly 90 percent of the world's animal life is found in the tropics, which include Guyana. Only mammals seem to be limited in number and variety, though

Sparse grasses and shrub vegetation characterize the savanna regions of Guyana.

Manatees, an endangered species, eat water plants and have become useful in unclogging irrigation channels and transportation sea-lanes. Once hunted for their flesh, hides, and blubber oil, manatees now enjoy international protection.

Tapirs inhabit the thick vegetation of the rain-forest, feeding on leaves, fruits, and plants.

often their shy manner or nighttime habits—and not their small numbers—keep them from being noticed.

Along the coast are numerous shore birds, including ducks, snipes, plovers, and herons, while inland streams host ibis and kingfishers. In the forests, swarms of brilliant-hued macaws make their homes, while other parrots abound in the savanna.

Among the vegetation of the river banks, sloths cling upside-down to the tree trunks. With their four-inch claws, giant anteaters tear at the concrete-hard surfaces of tall anthills in search of food. Manatees, or sea cows, thrive, growing to 12 feet in length and weighing as much as 1,500 pounds. Among the largest native mammals in South America, manatees have been over-hunted for their flesh and are now endangered animals.

Another animal that has been hunted almost to the point of extinction is the tapir. Related both to the horse and rhinoceros, the tapir is the largest and strangest-looking land animal in Guyana. The heavily hunted capybara is a piglike rodent that grows up to four feet in length and weighs as much as 100 pounds. Other animals that are exploited as food sources include peccaries—small wild pigs that

The city of Georgetown is located a few feet below sea level, which has made it necessary to build drainage canals and seawalls to keep out water.

often travel in groups of over 100—and several varieties of deer that graze on savanna grasses.

Guyana's rivers teem with fish, including the giant arapaima, a large freshwater fish. Flesh-eating piranhas are found in most streams, though their presence does not prevent the Guyanese from swimming. Verified accounts, however, of these small fish devouring both people and livestock in minutes have been documented.

Cities

Georgetown—named for Britain's eighteenth-century king George III—is Guyana's only large city, in addition to being the capital of the nation. With a population of 200,000, Georgetown lies near the mouth of the Demerara River and is Guyana's chief port. The capital displays wide streets laid out in a gridlike pattern, and some of the broader boulevards have small streams running through the middle of them. The business district parallels the river, while the government offices are grouped in the center of town. Most houses and other buildings are constructed of wood and are often perched on brick piers or stilts to raise them above the damp ground.

No other cities or towns rival the importance of Georgetown. Smaller settlements, such as New Amsterdam and Linden (formerly Mackenzie), provide other regions with their own focal point. New Amsterdam is an old Dutch town in northeastern Guyana on the east bank of the Berbice River. Like Georgetown, which is about 55 miles away, New Amsterdam has houses that are raised above the ground to guard against damage from flooding. As a port city, New Amsterdam ships sugar, rice, cattle products, and lumber brought in from the counties of East and West Berbice. Linden, on the other hand, is a new settlement, linked to the capital city by a good road. The town lies 70 miles up the Demerara River and is principally involved in bauxite mining, which is now a government-run activity.

An aerial view of Georgetown reveals its geometric street pattern.

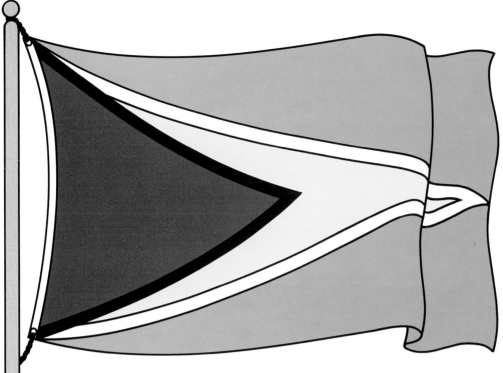

Upon achieving independence in 1966, the Guyanese introduced a new flag. The green background symbolizes agriculture and forests, the golden arrowhead represents mineral wealth, and the white border stands for water resources. The red triangle edged in black signifies the energy and zeal of the Guyanese in building their nation.

2) History and Government

Before the arrival of the Europeans, Guyana was inhabited by several native groups. The largest group was the Caribs, who lived in the upper reaches of the Essequibo River, as well as near the Mazaruni, Cuyuni, Pomeroon, and Barima rivers. The Caribs roamed the heavily forested regions of the interior.

Between the Courantyne and Waini rivers lived the Arawaks, a friendly, peace-loving tribe whose people were the first to greet Christopher Columbus in other areas of the Caribbean. Another native group, the Warrau, inhabited the swampland near the mouth of the Orinoco in present-day Venezuela but eventually moved east into Guyanese territory.

All of these peoples hunted and fished for their livelihoods. Some slept in skillfully crafted hammocks, and many built canoes to travel up and down Guyana's rivers.

Early Exploration

Christopher Columbus, during his third voyage to the New World in 1498, was the first European known to have sailed along the coast of Guyana. But Columbus only viewed the low-lying tropical shore. It was not until 1499 that Alonso de Ojeda became the first Spaniard to actually set foot on land. No settlement, however, resulted from this early exploration.

When European explorers landed on Guyana's coast, the local inhabitants were mainly of the Carib, Arawak, and Warrau tribes. The Arawaks lived in settled farming communities and slept in hammocks woven from strong fibers.

Born in Devonshire in 1554, Sir Walter Raleigh was famous not only as an explorer but also as an intellectual figure at the English court. During his last expedition in search of El Dorado in 1616, Raleigh sent his son Walter into the uncharted land of Guyana, where he was killed during an attack on a Spanish settlement.

At the time, the wealth-hungry Spaniards did not consider the scattered Caribs, Arawaks, and Warrau to be of any use. Initial contacts with these peoples had failed to provide the Spanish with any evidence of mineral wealth in the region. Consequently, the Spaniards made little effort to subdue and exploit the native groups, although the conquerors did enslave local populations in other parts of South America.

Furthermore, the relatively hospitable climate and topography of the lands that the Spaniards had already successfully colonized elsewhere in the Americas made Guyana, by comparison, unattractive. The seemingly impenetrable barriers of coastal mangrove swamps and of low-lying marshlands made the territory appear useless for agriculture or settlement. Moreover, navigation was extremely hazardous due to vast coastal mud flats and dangerous sandbars in the rivers and the ocean.

El Dorado

El Dorado was a mythical land based on the legend of an Indian leader who adorned his body with gold dust each morning and washed it off in a large lake each evening. This area was said to be located in the tropics of northern South America.

Not until 1593 was the search for El Dorado concentrated in the Guyana region. During that year, an ill-fated Spanish expedition of 2,000 people headed by Pedro da Silva searched in vain for the hidden golden land. Fewer than 50 people survived the ordeal of the search, whose participants had focused their attention on the Orinoco region.

Between 1595 and 1616, the Englishman Sir Walter Raleigh led three expeditions to the Guyana territory in search of El Dorado. Although Raleigh failed to locate any gold, his efforts resulted in the first mapping of the Guyanese coastline. He also established friendly contact with the region's Indians and described the area's

Independent Picture Service

natural attractions in his book, *Discoverie of the Large Riche and Bewtiful Empyre of Guiana.*

Dutch Colonization

The Dutch, who had been under Spain's domination since the mid-sixteenth century and who had recently broken away, were the first Europeans to gain a real foothold in Guyana. The Dutch were interested in securing good farmland on which they could raise tropical crops. The location, however, had to be easily defended against Spanish attack.

In 1616 Dutch colonists selected a site on an island bluff overlooking the junction of the Mazaruni and Cuyuni rivers, about 40 miles upstream from the mouth of the Essequibo. The settlement was named Kijk-over-al (Overlooking All). Early attempts at farming included the growing of coffee, tobacco, and cotton. Lack of an adequate work force to clear large tracts of

Dutch fears of Spanish invasion made protective measures—such as powerful cannons—essential in colonial times.

Independent Picture Service

24

land and to work the fields kept these initial agricultural experiments at a survival level.

Meanwhile in Europe, the Dutch States-General, which governed the provinces that would become Holland, granted a charter over the Guiana territory to the Dutch West India Company in 1621. The charter gave the company complete political and economic authority, the privilege to undertake pirate raids against Spanish shipping, and the right to carry slaves from West Africa to the New World. In terms of subsequent farm growth and development, the importation of slaves was essential. It also, however, clearly demonstrated a severe abuse of human rights.

Dutch Expansion

With a slave labor force, which consisted of men and women forcibly removed from their homes in Africa, the farms began to grow in size and in yield. The success of the Dutch venture encouraged the development of plantations in other inland regions of Guyana. Similar settlements appeared at the navigational boundaries for vessels along the Berbice, Demerara, and

The Dutch brought large numbers of African slaves into Guyana in the seventeenth century.

Pomeroon rivers. The Berbice district became a separate territory in 1732, and a Demerara district was established in 1741.

Several factors, however, brought about a gradual coastward movement of Dutch settlers. Other South American colonies were increasing the competition in the cotton and tobacco markets, but crops on the infertile soils of the Guyana interiors had begun to fail. Furthermore, since the threat of Spanish attack had diminished, valuable sugarcane, which had been introduced into the colony in 1637, could be grown safely on the fertile soils of the coastal plain.

Developing the coastal plains' low-lying and poorly drained land required capital (the initial investment of money), cooperation, and a large labor force. Also needed was something for which the Dutch were already famous—poldering—a vast system of irrigation and drainage works that reclaimed land from the sea. Poldering required the construction of an elaborate network of dikes, floodgates (called *ko-*

Based on methods introduced by the Dutch, this *koker,* or floodgate, at Anna Regina controls the flow of water from the sea.

Many present-day areas of Guyana are protected from flood damage by extensive seawalls that were constructed during the colonial period.

Stabroek Market—an example of the Dutch influence in Guyana—is a major landmark in the capital city of Georgetown.

kers), and irrigation and drainage canals. Only wealthy colonists could afford such undertakings, which resulted in the establishment of fewer and much larger plantations. The plantation owners held a virtual monopoly on sugar and tobacco production within the colony.

During this period of rapid expansion Laurens Storm van's Gravesande, director general of the Essequibo and Demerara districts, provided energetic leadership. He encouraged the further opening up of the Demerara lands and the movement of planters to the shores of the Essequibo. Such developments proved essential to the future of Guyana's agricultural capacity and even of its mining potential. Gravesande's contributions over a period of 30 years established him as the most important figure in the early history of Guyana.

In 1781 war broke out between the Dutch and the British over ownership of the colony and resulted in a year of British control over Guyana. A year later, the French seized power and governed for two years, during which time they created the new town of Longchamps at the mouth of the Demerara River. When the Dutch regained power in 1784, they moved their colonial capital to Longchamps and renamed it Stabroek. Later the settlement would be known as Georgetown.

Slavery

The history of Guyana has been closely linked to sugar. Clearing land for vast sugarcane fields and constructing vital flood-protection and drainage networks have always required a large work force. The introduction of slaves from Africa to perform this labor began on a massive scale under the 1621 charter of the Dutch West India Company. By 1770 more than 15,000 Africans were enslaved in Guyana. Nearly all of these slaves labored under the

27

Captured and sold to merchants in West Africa, enslaved laborers were forced to endure cramped living quarters and inadequate food while en route to the New World. Slaves continued to arrive in Guyana into the nineteenth century.

company's monopoly. At the height of the plantation period in the early nineteenth century, the slave population numbered more than 100,000 people.

The cruel conditions imposed on the black labor force caused frequent rebellions. In 1763 a house slave named Cuffy headed the most famous revolt, which he led from Magdalenenburg Plantation on the banks of the Canje River in Berbice district. Cuffy's immediate goal was to obtain more humane treatment for slaves, though his long-range objective was the total elimination of slavery. For nearly a year, the Africans controlled Berbice, but eventually Berbice's governor van Hoogenheim suppressed the revolt, in which more than 4,000 plantation owners and overseers had been killed. Cuffy is revered in Guyana's history as a national hero for his early role in the cause of freedom.

Arrival of British Planters

Beginning in the mid-eighteenth century, British planters from the West Indies were attracted to the fertile lands of the Demerara region. Even before their country won the colony from the Dutch, potential British colonists were offered a 10-year tax exemption and an initial grant of 250 acres of land as inducements to immigrate to Guyana. After clearing and planting this first 250 acres, new settlers were allowed to expand their plantations inland, rather than along the coast. Thus, sugar plantations evolved as long, narrow strips of land reaching from the coast toward the interior.

By 1760 the British made up more than half of Demerara's European population. By the 1780s, their numbers throughout Guyana were so great that the Dutch colony was effectively under British influence long before the British were formally ceded the territory.

British Rule

The Dutch maintained control over the Essequibo, Demerara, and Berbice settlements until 1796, when a British fleet from the Caribbean island of Barbados conquered the country. The British governed until 1802, at which time Guyana was restored to the Dutch under a truce established by the Treaty of Amiens.

In 1803 the British once again conquered the colony, which was finally ceded to them in 1814 under agreements contained in the

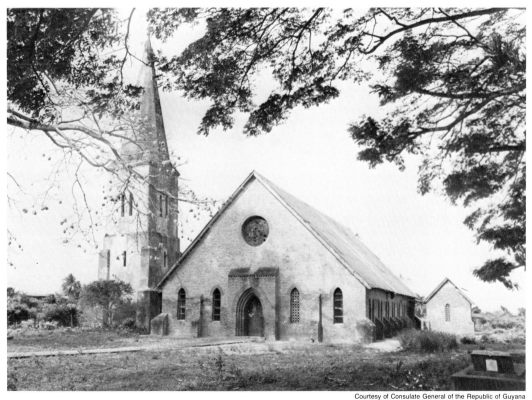

British settlers founded St. Peter's Church almost 200 years ago on Leguan Island at the mouth of the Essequibo River.

Treaty of Paris and the Congress of Vienna. European discord over the Guianas finally ended. The French secured French Guiana, the Dutch took over the territory of present-day Suriname, and the British paid the Dutch the equivalent of $15 million for Britain's slice of the Guiana region. Berbice continued under its own administration until 1831, when it was united with Essequibo and Demerara to form British Guiana.

Under British rule, trade and population increased rapidly. The capital city—renamed Georgetown after the British king George III—was modernized. Greater emphasis was placed on education, evidenced by the building of many schools and libraries. The British continued the Dutch project that reclaimed land from the sea. They also began to construct much needed roads, bridges, canals, and a railway.

Abolition of Slavery

In 1807 the slave trade was abolished throughout the British Empire. Planters could keep the slaves they owned at the time but could not buy new ones. Faced with the probable loss of field workers, the plantation owners undertook a deliberate scheme of slave breeding in an attempt to ensure an ongoing supply of labor.

By an act of the British parliament, slavery was abolished on August 1, 1834, throughout the British colonies. Thereafter, freed slaves were to be subject to a four-year apprenticeship, during which they were to be paid wages, housed, and clothed in exchange for their services. Final and complete emancipation was to be achieved in August 1838. Planters were to be compensated in the amount of 50 British pounds (about $250) for each slave they claimed as their property.

After emancipation, few former slaves chose to work—even for wages—for the plantation owners who had once enslaved them. Consequently, production declined drastically, falling by three-fifths between

In 1856 this stamp was issued in British Guiana—a colony that resulted from the unification of three former Dutch districts.

1839 and 1842. Ten years after the abolition of slavery, the number of plantations had dropped from 230 to 180. Only 16 of the 174 coffee and cotton plantations were still in operation.

The Indenture System

Faced with a critical shortage of workers, planters desperately searched for another system that would provide an abundance of low-wage labor. The landowners decided to import workers under a system of indentured servitude. This arrangement meant that in return for free passage to British Guiana, a person signed a contract to work for a fixed number of years. Usually only the provision of basic needs and a meager wage were offered in exchange for the labor.

Immigrants under this system included people from Portugal, China, the West Indies, and Africa. There were still not enough laborers, however. A wealthy plantation owner named John Gladstone proposed that workers be brought from the eastern regions of India to work on the plantations. The first East Indian immigrants arrived in 1838, but it was not until 1844 that they began to come in large numbers.

The East Indians were subject to a five-year indenture period. After five years they were free to return to India at their own expense. After a ten-year period of service, the government paid for passage back to their homeland.

Colonial Imbalance of Power

No matter how much headway was achieved by blacks or by indentured laborers, the reins of political power were still in the firm grasp of a European elite. Indeed, in 1850 only 916 qualified voters were counted out of a population of 130,000. Neither former slaves nor indentured workers could claim any political influence.

Toward the end of the nineteenth century, the imbalance of this political arrangement became intolerable to both blacks and East Indians, who together formed the bulk of the population. In 1891 the working class of British Guiana sent a petition to Britain's reigning queen Victoria to ask for representation in the British government. The government's response was to increase the power of the appointed colonial governor, at the expense of the power of the Combined Council, which was dominated by the plantation owners. Although this action reduced the control of the wealthy, British Guiana was still a long way from anything resembling a democratic form of government.

Border Disputes

In the mid-nineteenth century, Britain had sent German explorer Robert Hermann Schomburgk to define the borders of its Guiana colony. His boundaries included territories that both Brazil and Venezuela had traditionally called their own. In 1880 gold was discovered within the area claimed by both British Guiana and Venezuela. Not surprisingly, a dispute arose over true ownership of the land.

Courtesy of Patricia Koopmans

After the abolition of slavery, field workers on sugarcane plantations were scarce. Freed slaves abandoned large plantations, and the crops went unharvested. This situation caused British planters to set up the indenture system to provide low-cost agricultural laborers.

In the late nineteenth century, U.S. president Grover Cleveland involved the United States in a land dispute between British Guiana and Venezuela.

At the time, Great Britain was a strong imperial power, and Venezuela was comparatively weak. Consequently, Venezuela asked an eager United States to get involved. The U.S. president then was Grover Cleveland, who firmly believed in the Monroe Doctrine (a U.S. statement that warned against European interference in the Western Hemisphere). Cleveland sent messages to Great Britain demanding that Britain allow the border dispute to be settled with U.S. help. The British prime minister Lord Salisbury rejected the suggestion. Cleveland angrily threatened war, and Great Britain eventually agreed to submit its claim to an international commission. The commission—made up of two Venezuelans, two British, and one Russian—moved the boundaries slightly but awarded ownership of the disputed area largely to British Guiana.

The Twentieth Century

The indenture system, which had satisfied the planter aristocracy's demand for work-

ers, was abolished in British Guiana in 1917. During this same period, trade unions established a strong foothold under the leadership of Hubert Critchlow in the newly formed British Guiana Labour Union. Trade unionism had become a powerful force in Great Britain—as well as within its colonies—and in 1928 the British government ordered all of its dependencies to recognize the unions.

In the same year, the planter-dominated Combined Council was scrapped in favor of a one-house legislature. Nevertheless, only a small minority of colonists qualified as voters. Most policy decisions were settled in faraway London and carried out by a crown-appointed governor. In fact, political parties were not legal in British Guiana until 1940, and women were not allowed to vote until 1945.

Labor laws protecting skilled workers—such as shoemakers—began to have an impact in the early twentieth century. Hubert Critchlow, the principal force behind trade unionism in the Caribbean, focused his early efforts on fighting for better wages and safer working conditions in British Guiana.

The Road to Independence

Guyana's road to independence was a rocky one. In 1953 a new constitution granted all adult citizens the right to vote and established a two-house legislature. But political turmoil followed the first general election. The British government feared the Communist leanings of the winning People's Progressive party (PPP) led by Cheddi Jagan. In addition to the PPP's Communist stance, the party also advocated independence from Great Britain. Consequently, the British suspended the new constitution and the elected government.

From 1954 until new elections were held in 1957, an interim government ruled British Guiana. Meanwhile, Jagan, an East Indian, and his fellow PPP member Forbes Burnham, an African, had had a disagreement. Burnham left the PPP in 1957 and formed the People's National Congress (PNC), which eventually became an opposition party to the PPP. The split weakened the party's majority, but the PPP still won the most legislative seats in 1957 and again in 1961.

The new constitution was finally put into effect in 1961. Jagan was elected prime minister in 1962. Afro-Guyanese

As head of the People's Progressive party, Cheddi Jagan served as prime minister of the colonial Guyanese government from 1957 to 1964. In the 1980s he continued to lead the main minority party in the national legislature. In 1992, the PPP again won a legislative majority, and Jagan rose to the presidency.

Courtesy of Patricia Koopmans

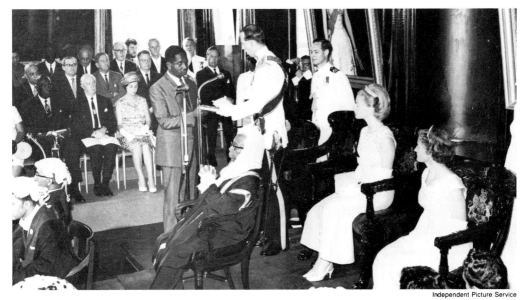

In 1966 Forbes Burnham *(standing left)* took the documents of independence from Britain's Duke of Kent *(standing right),* who represented his cousin Queen Elizabeth II in the ceremonies marking the transfer of sovereignty from Great Britain to Guyana.

As part of the Independence Day activities of May 26, 1966, soldiers raised the new Guyanese flag—called the Golden Arrowhead—for the first time.

fears of East Indian domination, however, sparked widespread riots in Georgetown. British troops arrived, a general strike broke out, and months of chaos followed. In a heavily contested election in 1964, the colonial governor declared Burnham the victor by virtue of his ability to lead a coalition of the PNC and the United Force, a third party. Together, these parties toppled the Jagan government.

Guyana Under Forbes Burnham

Throughout these unsettled years, British Guiana was still a colony. The nation's long struggle for independence ended in 1966 when Forbes Burnham assumed office as prime minister of independent Guyana. But the struggles to gain independence were followed by internal abuses of power. Reportedly rigged elections consolidated Burnham's control but lost the prime minister (later the president) much of his grass-roots support. Nevertheless, Burnham ruled Guyana for 19 years until his death in office in August 1985.

Independence Arch was presented as a gift to the nation by the foreign-owned **Demerara Bauxite Company**, which has since been nationalized and renamed the Guyana Mining Enterprise.

This monument to the four founders of the nonaligned movement – displayed at Georgetown's Company Path Garden – depicts *(left to right)* President Gamal Abdel Nasser of Egypt, President Kwame Nkrumah of Ghana, Prime Minister Jawaharlal Nehru of India, and President Josef Tito of Yugoslavia.

35

To put an end to foreign meddling in Guyanese affairs, Burnham steadfastly kept Guyana among the world's non-aligned nations in world affairs. Moreover, under Burnham's leadership, Guyana declared itself a cooperative republic in 1970. Guyana became a socialist nation, in which natural resources, business enterprises, and the government were to be managed cooperatively.

Under Burnham the Guyanese government also nationalized its industries—including foreign-owned bauxite companies—which produced much of the country's wealth. By 1985 more than three-quarters of the country's economy had been brought under government control.

Recent Events

Immediately following Burnham's death in 1985, the vice president, Hugh Desmond Hoyte, was sworn into office. Regularly scheduled elections—criticized by many observers as fraudulent—were held in December of 1985. Hoyte and the PNC won a solid victory, which many people regarded as an indication that little in Guyanese politics had changed.

The Guyanese government carried out important electoral reforms in the early 1990s. New voter lists were prepared to replace former, fraudulent lists. Voting in October 1992 brought the PPP back to power, and Cheddi Jagan again became the president. The PPP won a one-member majority in the legislature. Guyana's new government has announced that it will reform the economy, attempt to reduce the nation's heavy debt, and bring inflation under control. The government has also announced plans to revise the constitution. But ethnic conflict remains a serious issue, with the principle political parties drawing on the two major ethnic groups for their support. With only a slim majority, the PPP may face difficulties in carrying out important changes and reforms.

In 1985 Hugh Desmond Hoyte succeeded Forbes Burnham as president of Guyana. Here, Hoyte addresses the Guyanese legislature.

Brightly decorated buildings are included in the festivities in honor of Republic Day, which marks Guyana's emergence as a socialist nation in 1970.

Guyana's chief executive lives in a large, wood-framed house in a quiet section of Georgetown.

Government

Guyana's first independently administered constitution became effective on May 26, 1966—Guyanese Independence Day. In February 1970 Guyana declared itself a sovereign democratic republic and thereby ended its ties with the British crown.

In accordance with a new constitution, which took effect in October 1980, a president (rather than a prime minister) heads the government. A separate, one-house national assembly of 65 members is elected to five-year terms. Because the president is the leader of the majority party in the legislature, the presidential term lasts for the duration of the assembly. The president appoints the cabinet, which may include ministers who are not elected members of the assembly.

Although the constitution is the supreme law of the land, Guyana also has two legal traditions—British common law and the Dutch code. Magistrate courts handle small monetary claims, and a higher court has jurisdiction in civil and criminal matters.

Guyana is made up of 10 regions. A Regional Democratic Council administers each region. Each council elects a representative to the national assembly.

Guyanese students run to the playground from their schoolhouse, which is constructed on high stilts to guard against damage during the flood season.

3) The People

"One people, one nation, one destiny" reads the motto on Guyana's coat of arms. Achieving this goal with such an ethnically diverse population sometimes has been a violent undertaking. The population, which numbered approximately 730,000 in the mid-1990s, consists mostly of people of East Indian (50 percent) or of African (30 percent) ancestry. Nevertheless, Chinese, Portuguese, British, and Amerindian peoples all have contributed to the cultural heritage of the land. (The name Amerindians is used for Guyana's native groups to distinguish them from the immigrant East Indian population.)

The nation's socially elite population consists mostly of wealthy Guyanese of European, East Indian, African, and Portuguese descent. The middle-income group is not well defined, and social mobility is related more to occupation than to ethnic identity. Guyanese of East Indian and

This woman—part of Guyana's small population of Amerindians—makes a grater by putting notches in a smooth board.

African backgrounds who do manual labor are part of the lower-income groups, while the original inhabitants of Guyana— the Amerindians—tend to remain outside the nation's visible social stream.

Ethnic Groups

In Guyana the dominant people political-ly and culturally are the Afro-Guyanese, who are descended mainly from slaves brought from the Guinea coast of West Africa in the seventeenth, eighteenth, and nineteenth centuries. Survivors of a trans-planted African heritage, these Guyanese have largely adopted the European culture and Christian religion, which colonists brought with them to the New World.

Within urban areas, Guyanese blacks often participate in the nation's growing fish industry, by either catching (left) or packing (above) the seafood.

39

Some Afro-Guyanese live in small villages and farming communities, but most dwell in towns or in the capital city.

Most Guyanese of East Indian background claim the Ganges Valley of northern India and various parts of southern India as the source of their cultural roots. The first arrivals came over as indentured laborers, and their descendants—who generally live in rural areas—now make up half of the Guyanese population. Three major Indian languages—Hindi, Tamil, and Telugu—are still in use among East Indian Guyanese, although only about 2 percent can write these Indian tongues. The East Indians and Africans limit contact with one another as a result of the violent political clashes that occurred between them from 1962 to 1964.

More than 30,000 Amerindians still live in Guyana and are descendants of the

Courtesy of Inter-American Development Bank

Amerindians—who historically have not been involved in Guyana's development—are beginning to enter the commercial and social mainstream. This man has a job as a dockworker in Georgetown.

Courtesy of Patricia Koopmans

The strong presence of the Indian culture is illustrated by a group of Hindu dancers.

earliest inhabitants of northeastern South America. Each of a dozen native groups speaks a different dialect of Carib, Arawak, or Warrau tongues. Of the various racial and cultural groups represented in Guyana, the Amerindians are the least integrated into the social, political, and economic activities of the nation.

Most native groups inhabit isolated areas in the interior or in the more remote coastal regions. These groups still cling to many of their traditional practices. Other Amerindians, however, have partly accepted European ways to the extent that they wear Western clothing, take advantage of modern technology, and often work on cattle ranches or in the mines. Efforts by missionaries and various government agencies have brought about greater involvement of the Amerindians in recent decades.

With a Brahman priest *(far right)* officiating, a bride *(in yellow)* and groom *(in pink)* exchange their wedding vows.

Many Amerindians still live in isolated settlements in the interior of the country. An aerial view illustrates how well-hidden one such community is by the rain-forest that surrounds it.

A Hindu temple *(left)* and a Muslim mosque *(below)* represent two of Guyana's principal religions.

Religion

Religious freedom is guaranteed by the Guyanese constitution, but most of the people are classified as Christian. Thirty-five percent are Hindu, and 9 percent are Muslim, who adhere to the Islamic faith. Primarily because of ambitious missionary activities during the nineteenth century, the Afro-Guyanese are mostly Christian, as are nearly all citizens of European and Chinese descent. Eighteen percent of the population is Roman Catholic, and 16 percent is Anglican. The major religious holidays of each of the three faiths—Christianity, Hinduism, and Islam—are observed nationally.

St. George's Cathedral—said to be one of the tallest wooden buildings in the world—serves the Anglican community of Georgetown.

Obeahism, with rituals that descend from African voodoo, is outlawed but still flourishes in secret. In Guyana, Obeahmen and Obeahwomen are believed to have the power to call upon spirits through magic. Among the tools of the Obeah practitioners are bones, blood, ashes, feathers, and old rags. People seek out Obeahmen and Obeahwomen to cure disease, to discover their enemies, to bring about success in love, to seek revenge, or to experience good luck in employment or financial dealings. The practices are common among both the African and East Indian populations, though Amerindians and some Europeans are also believers.

Religious cults have found enthusiastic followers in Guyana and have sometimes been led by foreigners. The cult known as People's Temple began in California and consisted of U.S. citizens under the leadership of Reverend Jim Jones. Members of the Guyanese government found Jones's credentials sound and his well-funded building project persuasive. Authorities granted Jones permission to construct a religious center in Guyana's western regions, near Port Kaituma. The enterprise ended in tragedy, however. Investigations begun in the United States revealed cause for concern over Jones's methods of religious recruitment. Before the investigations were completed, the entire community of almost 1,000 people committed mass suicide in 1978 at Jones's order.

Education

About 96 percent of the Guyanese population is literate—one of the highest rates

Guyanese students concentrate on their lessons. Educational standards in Guyana are higher than in some other developing nations.

Under the banner "With Agriculture We Will Survive," schoolchildren form a circular parade at an outdoor festival.

in the Western Hemisphere. English is the official language, but Amerindian dialects and East Indian tongues are spoken as well. Primary education is compulsory and free for citizens between the ages of 6 and 14 years. More than 400 primary schools, staffed by more than 6,000 teachers, accommodate nearly 165,000 pupils. Secondary education is available in almost 90 schools, but only about 57 percent of the primary school students go on to high school.

Fifteen technical institutes provide vocational education. The curricula of these institutions are heavily weighted toward engineering, construction, and related practical studies. Founded in 1962, the University of Guyana occupies a modern campus in the Georgetown suburb of Turkeyen. The university has an enrollment of almost 2,000 students and offers programs of study in the arts, natural and social sciences, agriculture, technology, education, business, and public administration.

Sports

Cricket and, secondarily, volleyball are the most popular team activities in Guyana. Schools, local groups, and professional clubs all organize volleyball teams. Cricket, a sport largely unknown to most people in the United States, has a somewhat distant resemblance to baseball. The sport is played in Britain and throughout the former British colonial world—in Africa, India, and the West Indies—with great enthusiasm.

Cricket teams consist of 11 members, but the game's main action is between a bowler (like a pitcher) and a batsman (akin to a batter). The bowler throws the ball to the batsman, who attempts to hit it with the bat. If the player does, and if the ball goes to the edge of or outside of the boundaries of the field, the player scores points, called runs. If the ball is caught, the player is considered out and batting for that player is concluded. The player continues to bat until he or she has been called out—an

A Guyanese bowler *(left)* throws his overhand pitch to a waiting—and fully padded—batsman *(below)*.

Courtesy of Patricia Koopmans

Courtesy of Patricia Koopmans

Courtesy of Patricia Koopmans

Along with cricket and football (soccer), volleyball engages the enthusiasm of Guyanese athletes. Here, a school team in Anna Regina takes on visiting players from Bartica.

event that can take hours to occur. Individual batting scores of 100 runs (called centuries) are notable but not uncommon.

After all 11 batsmen have come to bat—which represents half of an inning—the teams switch activities to complete the inning. Since the teams each have two innings at bat, a cricket match can easily take more than a day to complete.

Literature and the Arts

Guyana has long provided a theme for literary expression. Well-known novels relating to the Guyana region include Sir Arthur Conan Doyle's *The Lost World* and William Henry Hudson's *Green Mansions.*

Native authors whose works are popular include Wilson Harris, Jan Carew, Denis Williams, Christopher Nicole, and E. R. Braithwaite. Braithwaite's memoir *To Sir With Love* details his experiences as a black high school teacher in a white London slum. The work was praised for its hopeful view of difficult race relations and became the subject of a major motion picture.

Edgar Mittelholzer, a member of a Guyanese family of Swiss origin, is well known outside of his native country for such nov-

Courtesy of Consulate General of the Republic of Guyana

At the Vanceram factory a craftswoman hand paints tableware made of local clays.

Independent Picture Service

Guyanese artist Aubrey Williams captures a tense mood in his painting entitled *Revolt.*

Courtesy of Consulate General of the Republic of Guyana

Guyana's National Dance Company—a multiethnic troupe—performs intricate East Indian steps.

els as *Corentyne Thunder* and a three-part novel known as the Kaywana trilogy. The latter set of stories focuses on one family through 350 years of Guyana's history. *Miramy,* a full-length Guyanese comedy by Frank Pilgrim, is set on an imaginary island in the West Indies. It became the first locally written play to be performed overseas.

Art takes many forms in Guyana, but its dominant themes are the Amerindians, the ethnic diversity of the population, and the physical beauties of Guyana. The works of Stanley Greaves, Ronald Savory, Emerson Samuels, Philip Moore, and Aubrey Williams have been much in demand in the last two decades. Savory's works, in particular, have brought the hard-to-reach Guyanese interior within view of urban dwellers.

A fast-paced African rhythm provides the tempo for these festively dressed Guyanese dancers.

Courtesy of Inter-American Development Bank

At a wedding, women busily prepare puris, which are light, fried wheat cakes of Indian origin that are often eaten as a dessert.

A national food fair displays the variety of Guyana's fruits and vegetables.

48

Food

One of the most distinct expressions of cultural diversity is found in the foods people eat. Each of Guyana's ethnic groups has contributed foods that have become a regular part of Guyanese dining habits. English roast beef, puddings, and tea appear with Indian curries, Chinese noodles, and chow mein. Portuguese garlic pork and African *metemgee* may also appear on the table.

In rural areas, the diet is simpler than it is in urban regions. A rural family begins the day with tea—a light meal of bread and margarine, sometimes accompanied by a brew made from the leaves of the soursop (a tropical fruit). Breakfast—the main meal of the day—is served at 11:30 A.M., and usually consists of rice, potatoes, and fish or meat. Suppertime is at 5:30 or 6:00 P.M. and may include rice and bits of pork.

Health

In recent years, public health standards have improved somewhat throughout Guyana. In the early 1990s, the country's infant mortality rate of 48 deaths in every 1,000 live births was just above the South American average of 46 per 1,000. The life expectancy figure of 65 years of age, however, is among the lowest figures in South America.

A network of public and private hospitals and other medical facilities, including rural maternal and child health units, is working to improve health conditions. These institutions not only provide basic medical care but also have taken an active role in nationwide, antidisease campaigns —against malaria, yellow fever, and AIDS, for example. The clinics promote community health education programs and train an increasing number of paramedical personnel. They have led the drive to bring pure drinking water to rural areas of Guyana.

Housing remains a critical problem. Many homes lack adequate sanitation and electricity. Slums are common both in Georgetown and on rural plantations. The government has accomplished little in the way of new housing construction, though ambitious plans have been publicized.

Athletic programs, which are heavily emphasized in Guyanese schools, help to make Guyana's youth healthy.

On a coastal plantation, two Guyanese workers remove the white meat from coconut shells. The meat will be used in making oil, and the husks are the raw material of a strong fiber.

4) The Economy

Guyana draws most of its wealth from its natural resources. Sugarcane and rice, as well as other valuable crops, thrive in Guyana's hot, wet climate. The country's forests are rich in valuable hardwoods, and underground there are extensive deposits of bauxite, the raw material from which aluminum is made.

At one time, Guyana had a balanced and well-tuned economy that depended upon agricultural products and mining resources. But after Guyana won its independence in the 1960s, the country experienced one of the fastest economic declines in modern history. The production of major exports—sugar, bauxite, and rice—fell, while inflation (rising prices) worsened. Payment on foreign debts claimed much of Guyana's export income.

Thousands of workers emigrated from the country, and state-owned businesses experienced a shortage of skilled workers.

In the early 1990s, the country's economic picture improved. The government lifted controls on prices and wages and began a program of privatization—selling state-owned companies to private investors. Guyana's gross domestic product (GDP)—a measure of productivity—rose sharply in 1993.

But in the mid-1990s, Guyana still faced a heavy foreign debt, a labor shortage, and falling production of important exports such as gold and bauxite. The country lacks important infrastructure, such as roads and port facilities, and has yet to develop its fishing and forestry into successful export businesses.

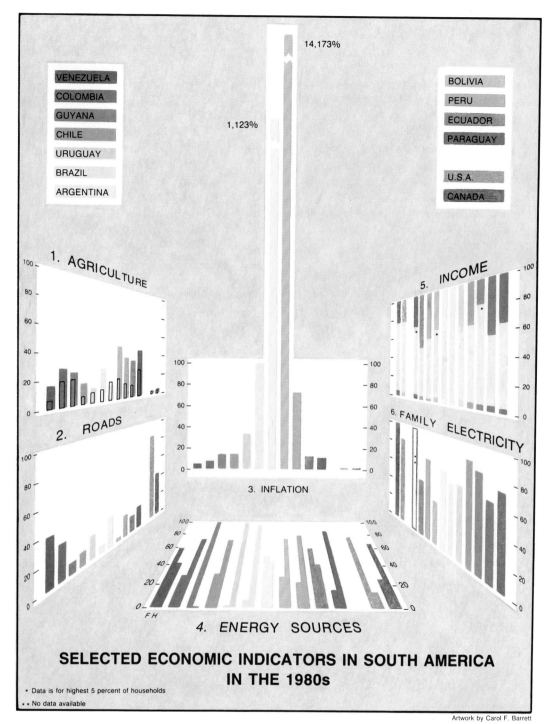

14,173%

1,123%

VENEZUELA
COLOMBIA
GUYANA
CHILE
URUGUAY
BRAZIL
ARGENTINA

BOLIVIA
PERU
ECUADOR
PARAGUAY

U.S.A.
CANADA

1. AGRICULTURE

5. INCOME

6. FAMILY ELECTRICITY

2. ROADS

3. INFLATION

4. ENERGY SOURCES

**SELECTED ECONOMIC INDICATORS IN SOUTH AMERICA
IN THE 1980s**

* Data is for highest 5 percent of households

** No data available

Artwork by Carol F. Barrett

This multigraph depicts six important South American economic factors. The same factors for the United States and Canada are included for comparison. Data is from *1986 Britannica Book of the Year, Encyclopedia of the Third World, Europa Yearbook,* and *Countries of the World and their Leaders, 1987.*

In GRAPH 1—labeled Agriculture—the colored bars show the percentage of a country's total labor force that works in agriculture. The overlaid black boxes show the percentage of a country's gross domestic product that comes from agriculture. In most cases—except Argentina —the number of agricultural workers far exceeds the amount of income produced by the farming industry.

GRAPH 2 depicts the percentage of paved roads, while GRAPH 3 illustrates the inflation rate. The inflation figures for Colombia, Guyana, and Brazil are estimated. GRAPH 4 depicts two aspects of energy usage. The left half of a country's bar is the percentage of energy from fossil fuel (oil or coal); the right half shows the percentage of energy from hydropower. In GRAPH 5, which depicts distribution of wealth, each country's bar represents 100 percent of its total income. The top section is the portion of income received by the richest 10 percent of the population. The bottom section is the portion received by the poorest 20 percent. GRAPH 6 represents the percentage of homes that have electricity. 34557

Agriculture

Agriculture is the mainstay of Guyana's economy, though less than one-quarter of the population is engaged in farming. Cash crops include sugarcane—from which rum and molasses, as well as sugar, are derived —rice, coffee, and cacao (from which chocolate is made). Production of sugarcane and rice, found mostly on the coastal plain, requires much manual labor. Agricultural production increased in the middle of the twentieth century. But labor strikes, unpredictable weather, pests, and scant supplies of fertilizer and farm equipment caused production to stagnate in the 1980s and early 1990s. Other food crops, also planted mostly on the fertile soil near the coast, include vegetables and citrus fruits.

SUGAR

Sugarcane is Guyana's major agricultural crop. Almost half of all farm workers are employed in raising and harvesting sugarcane. In the early 1990s this crop made up more than one third of the value of Guyana's exports to foreign countries.

Growing sugarcane is a big business that requires vast amounts of capital. Money is needed to maintain drainage and irrigation systems and to protect soil fertility. As a result, sugar production had been concentrated in the hands of several nationalized plantations. Under President Hoyte, approximately half of Guyana's sugarcane operations were handed over to private businesspeople.

Sugarcane cultivation is confined almost exclusively to a belt of land varying in width from two to eight miles along the coastal plain between the Courantyne and Essequibo rivers. The typical plantation has an ocean frontage protected by a seawall. The first mile from the sea may be used for growing rice or for pasture.

Courtesy of Patricia Koopmans

In a large rice field, workers separate the nutritious grains of rice from the stalks.

Independent Picture Service

Surrounded by tall, ripe stalks, a hardworking sugarcane cutter raises his machete, or knife, to fell another plant.

Farther inland, for distances of up to eight miles, the land is used to grow sugar. A back dam, located behind the cultivated area, keeps out swamp water and holds it for use until it is needed in the fields.

A method called flood fallowing is employed in the growing of sugarcane. The fields are tilled and then flooded for at least six months, after which they are drained and planted. This practice increases yields by as much as 40 percent and is unique to Guyana.

Once planted, sugarcane grows for a period of 12 to 18 months before reaching maturity. When the crop is ready for harvest, the 12-foot stalks are set on fire so that they can be cut by hand more easily. The stalks are piled in rows and transported to mills in flat-bottomed barges, which are towed along canals by oxen, mules, or tractors.

After the stalks have been cut, the root-stubble remains in the ground and produces new shoots called ratoons. After five years,

Independent Picture Service

Cut sugarcane stalks are transported to mills on barges that are pulled along canals by tractors or animals.

Workers harvest a rice crop by hand in a well-watered area west of the Demerara River.

the ratoon crops show decreasing yields and the fields are again flood fallowed.

RICE

Indentured plantation workers introduced rice production to Guyana. By the last decade of the nineteenth century, the grain had become a crop of commercial importance. Rice is now Guyana's second most important agricultural product. During a normal year, approximately 340,000 tons of rice are harvested. It is both the staple foodstuff of the country and an export product that generates just under eight percent of the export revenues.

Small-scale farmers plant over 250,000 acres of rice paddies. These farms average under five acres in size and are leased from large landholders or from the government, or they are individually owned. Nearly one-third of the total population depends upon rice cultivation for a living. More than twice as much land is devoted to rice as is given over to sugarcane.

The Guyana Rice Board Research Station developed this new variety of rice, called "rustic," which may increase crop yields.

Rice farms are now highly mechanized, with combines and tractors replacing hand tools and oxen. Water for flooding the paddies, which prevents the growth of weeds, comes from reservoirs located behind the back dams. The water travels to the paddies by way of an intricate network of irrigation canals. The heavy clay content of the soil prevents water loss through seepage.

Planting occurs at the beginning of the long rainy season in April or May, and the harvest takes place during the October dry season. In areas with extremely good soil, two crops may be grown each year. Yields normally exceed those of most Asian countries. The best lands produce up to 2,000 pounds of rice per acre, and the average throughout the country ranges from 60 to 75 percent of that figure.

LIVESTOCK

The livestock industry is hindered by the inaccessibility of the pasturelands and by the low nutritional value of the native

Courtesy of Consulate General of the Republic of Guyana

Corralled cattle wait to graze on savanna grasses of the Rupununi region. A weak industry in past years, livestock raising has gained new energy with improvements in pasturelands.

Courtesy of Patricia Koopmans

Picked and threshed rice is dried in the sun and packed in woven sacks. These bags are waiting to be collected for the journey to the mill.

The sparse grasslands of the Rupununi Savanna have discouraged efforts toward large-scale animal husbandry in the region.

At the government-run Guybau Mine *(above)*, machines remove the earth's upper layer of sand and clay to allow excavators to extract the bauxite ore. Bauxite varies in color from white to brown and collects in small lumps, usually about as big as a pea. The lumps are dumped into trucks *(below)* and are transported along Guyana's many rivers *(opposite top)* for further refining into alumina.

grasses. Periodic outbreaks of hoof-and-mouth disease have occurred, and vampire bats have transmitted rabies to the livestock. Consequently, beef production is barely sufficient to supply local needs.

The prospects for livestock raising are somewhat encouraging, however, due to the introduction of cattle breeds that are more resistant to tropical diseases and pests. The presence of these hardy breeds, such as Santa Gertrudis and zebu, has helped to eliminate hoof-and-mouth disease. The planting of more nutritious, imported grasses has also contributed to the growth in this segment of the economy. More than 190,000 cattle feed on pasturelands, mostly in the southern uplands.

Mining

Bauxite replaced sugar as Guyana's leading export in the 1970s. Bauxite production, which began in 1914, totaled 930,000 tons in 1992, making Guyana one of the world's leading producers of this ore. More than 90 percent of Guyana's annual production comes from the Linden region,

Independent Picture Service

located about 70 miles up the Demerara River. To mine bauxite, the ground's thick layer of white sand and clay is removed, and the ore is extracted from the exposed surface. Some ore still goes to the United States, but increasing amounts are shipped to Canada.

Even though El Dorado proved to be only a Spanish legend, gems and precious minerals such as gold have contributed substantially to the country's wealth. Guyana's need for the revenues it earns from gold may need to be balanced with the environmental risks of mining.

In August 1995, a spill at a gold-mining site emptied 3.5 million tons of cyanide-laced water into a tributary of the Essequibo River. As a result, gold production was temporarily shut down while the Guyanese government reviewed environmental conditions at the site.

Courtesy of Consulate General of the Republic of Guyana

A lone Guyanese prospector stands in waist-high water to pan for gold.

Guyana's rivers transport both cargo and passenger traffic between the country's towns and villages, some of which are not served by overland roads.

Transportation

Guyana depends largely on its waterways for transportation. As a result, in rural areas ferries and canoes perform the function that trucks, buses, and cars do in other countries. The nation's 180-mile-long main road extends along the Atlantic coast from Charity on the Pomeroon River to Corriverton on the Courantyne, near the border of Suriname. Two unbridged gaps occur at the Berbice and the Essequibo rivers, and the banks of the Demerara River are linked by a floating bridge. Only one good road extends inland, running for 50 miles between Linden and Georgetown. Foreign mining companies installed secondary railway track, such as the line between Linden and Ituni, to carry bauxite to rivers or roads for further transport.

Airplanes fly goods and people to otherwise inaccessible regions of Guyana, and

In isolated areas, such as the Rupununi, oxcarts are still in use as land transportation vehicles.

Guyana Airways has regular flights to more than 20 towns within the nation. The company also links Guyana with cities in the Caribbean and in North America.

regularly scheduled flights bring visitors to Kaieteur Falls or the Mazaruni diamond fields. The flights are organized by the national airline, Guyana Airways Corporation, whose main base is Timehri Airport about 25 miles upstream from Georgetown.

Within the many small villages and towns throughout Guyana, however, the most common form of modern transit is the bicycle. Paved roads in the interior are few, and flooding often stops movement, except on foot.

Passenger trains, once a popular form of transportation in Guyana, no longer exist along the coast. Most overland routes in the country are covered by bus and taxi services.

Forestry and Manufacturing

The timber industry is based upon the logging of valuable woods found within the rain-forests. Loggers encounter a number of difficulties in the cutting and transporting of timber. Foremost among these problems are the lack of concentrated stands of commercially valuable wood and inadequate roads in the forested areas. Other difficulties include the absence of uniform rules for grading the lumber, inadequate mills, and the shortage of shipping and storage space for exporters.

The major market demand has been for greenheart, a wood famous for its resistance to termites and decay. Areas bordering rivers have been heavily exploited. The remaining trees are either so young or so scattered that it may be more economical in the future to replace greenheart with treated wood from other species.

Most manufacturing is related to the processing of bauxite, timber, and agricultural products. Many consumer goods must still be imported, and the government has banned the importation of foods that it believes Guyana is able—but has yet—to produce itself. Canned fish, for example, is no longer an import item, despite the fact that Guyana's fish-processing industry is at best in a fledgling state. Guyana is almost totally dependent upon outside sources for heavy equipment, cars, and automotive products, including petroleum, household appliances, chemicals, textiles, foodstuffs—including milk and wheat flour—and the majority of its luxury items.

Courtesy of Inter-American Development Bank

Forests containing valuable woods cover more than four-fifths of Guyana's total land area. Here, loggers secure trees— recently cut from stands in central Guyana—to a transport truck.

Guyanese workers clean fish caught in coastal waters. The fish will eventually be made into processed food products.

The curing and packaging of hams and bacon is a strong and growing industry in Guyana.

A forester skillfully squares a freshly felled log. This operation prepares the wood for cutting into planks, which will then be used as building material.

In the 1970s, Guyana experienced a marked increase in the number of its light industries. Among the items these small-scale manufacturers produce are furniture, clothing, jewelry, cigarettes, soft drinks, bricks, soap, bacon, and ham.

Unemployment

Although official estimates are difficult to obtain, unemployment figures as high as 40 percent of the able population have been cited in Guyana. Unemployment has been worsened by food shortages, which affect people at the most basic level. Shortages and unemployment have resulted in mass emigrations and waves of violent crime. Guyana is losing many of its skilled and unskilled laborers, who seek a safer life and better jobs elsewhere. As a result, the country suffers a shortage of labor.

President Jagan's plans to reform the economy may attract more foreign investment and eventually help create more jobs for the Guyanese. Privatizing businesses

Courtesy of Patricia Koopmans

Interior parts of Guyana, including much of the rain-forest, have been claimed by Venezuela since the late nineteenth century.

Courtesy of Patricia Koopmans

Guyana's high unemployment rate will make it difficult for these secondary students to find jobs after leaving school.

In recent times, some dissatisfied Guyanese have emigrated in search of better living conditions and job opportunities.

and encouraging foreign investment may also lower unemployment rates and entice educated Guyanese to remain in or return to their country.

President Hugh Desmond Hoyte is head of the People's National Congress (PNC) party. The PNC controlled Guyana's government from 1966 until 1992, when the People's Progressive party (PPP) won a single-vote majority in the Guyanese legislature.

The Future

After years of corruption and mismanagement, Guyana's government must now concentrate on political and economic reforms. Free and fair elections are a sign that political reforms are in place and working. But the economy has a long way to go. Industrial development would depend on a reliable power supply. Guyana's energy sources, already overtaxed by aging equipment, are often shut down for most of the day – even in the nation's capital.

Another problem is Venezuela's claim to the Essequibo region, which comprises more than two-thirds of Guyana. In addition, Guyana's ethnic tensions still run high. Under President Hoyte, the number of East Indians holding high political office increased, helping to relax ethnic divisions. But the 1992 elections brought a return of conflict between Guyana's East Indian and Afro-Guyanese people. A strongly united population would help the Guyanese deal with the serious economic struggles of their uncertain future.

Index